Good Manners at Home

Thank you!

by Katie Marsico
illustrated by John Haslam
Content consultant: Robin Gaines Lanzi, PhD, MPH,
Department of Human Science, Georgetown University

visit us at www.abdopublishing.com

Published by Magic Wagon, a division of the ABDO Group, 8000 West 78th Street, Edina, Minnesota, 55439. Copyright © 2009 by Abdo Consulting Group, Inc. International copyrights reserved in all countries. All rights reserved. No part of this book may be reproduced in any form without written permission from the publisher.

Looking Glass Library™ is a trademark and logo of Magic Wagon.

Printed in the United States.

Text by Katie Marsico
Illustrations by John Haslam
Edited by Amy Van Zee
Interior layout and design by Becky Daum
Cover design by Becky Daum

Library of Congress Cataloging-in-Publication Data
Marsico, Katie, 1980-
  Good manners at home / by Katie Marsico ; illustrated by John Haslam.
     p. cm. — (Good manners matter!)
  Includes bibliographical references (p.   ).
  ISBN 978-1-60270-607-1
  1. Etiquette for children and teenagers. 2. Family—Juvenile literature. 3. Home—Juvenile literature. I. Haslam, John. II. Title.
  BJ1857.C5M1263 2009
  395.5—dc22

                          2008036315

Contents

Why Do Good Manners Matter at Home?

Your favorite television show is about to start. You watched it yesterday, too. You even have your popcorn ready. But, your older brother's favorite show is on a different channel. He didn't get to watch his show yesterday. How should you decide what show to watch?

You were right if you guessed that you should take turns. That means it's your brother's turn to watch his favorite show. This is one way you can practice good manners at home.

It would also be polite to share your popcorn! Sharing is a great way to show good manners. It lets others know that you are thinking of them.

There are many situations at home where manners are important. What would dinner be like without good manners? Imagine everyone talking at the same time at the dinner table. The dishes and food might not be cleaned up after the meal. You would probably wish you were eating somewhere else!

Do you know why it matters to have good manners at home? Good manners show respect for those around you. By using good manners, others will want to spend time with you. You'll also earn their respect. What are some good manners?

Manners are extra important when you meet someone new. You can show a new friend just how polite you are!

Show Good Manners at Home!

Taking turns is an important way to practice good manners at home. You and your brothers and sisters can take turns doing chores. You can take out the trash this week. Your sister can do the dishes. Then you can trade next week.

Sharing is another way to show good manners at home. Be sure to share your favorite things. Do you have a favorite food? Other people in your home might like that food, too. It's rude not to share with others.

Having good manners means showing respect.
You can show respect for everyone who lives in your house. You share space with these people. Keep this in mind if you leave a mess in the family room.
Your mom may be unhappy if she has to put away your toys.

Show respect for your parents by doing what you can to help around the house. You can also look to your parents for examples of good manners.

How else can you practice good manners at home? There are many ways to show how polite you are at the dinner table. Making a meal takes lots of work. Your parents will be grateful if you offer to help prepare the food. You can also set the table and clear the dishes when you're done.

Family meals are a chance for everyone to share their thoughts. This is why it's important to speak clearly and listen well. Never talk with your mouth full of food. This makes it hard for people to understand what you're saying. Don't talk while someone else at the table is speaking.

What should you do if you want the bowl of carrots that's in the middle of the table? Should you stretch your arm across someone's plate to reach the food? It's better manners to ask whoever is closest to the bowl to pass it to you. You should also ask, "May I be excused?" when you're ready to leave the table.

Other words that show you have good manners are "excuse me" and "you are welcome." You should also say "please" and "thank you." Home isn't the only place you should use good manners. You can practice good manners wherever you go. Now get ready to see some good manners in motion!

Don't worry about having perfect manners right away. The more you practice using good manners, the more natural they will become.

Manners in Motion

Carl had just gotten an A on his science test.
He couldn't wait to tell his family at dinner.

He and his sister, Sara, set the table. Then their mom
and dad brought out the pasta and salad. Both Carl
and Sara loved their parents' pasta.

"I got an A on my science test," he told his family. They were all very happy for him.

"Nice work!" said Mom. "Carl, I see you've finished your pasta." Carl wanted more. The pasta bowl was near Sara.

"Sara, could you please pass the pasta?" he asked.

"Of course," answered Sara. She handed Carl the bowl.

"Thanks!" Carl said. He was careful about how much pasta he took. He wanted to be sure there was some left for Sara. He waited until he was done chewing before he spoke again.

"Sara, do you want to play checkers later?" Checkers was Sara's favorite game. They'd played hide-and-seek last night. That was Carl's favorite game.

"That'd be fun!" answered Sara. "We can play right after we clear the table."

Can you name all the different ways Carl and his family practiced good manners at home? Having good manners is easy! Just remember to be polite and show respect for your family members. What good manners have you practiced at home lately?

Amazing Facts about Manners at Home

Please Take Off Your Shoes!

Do you wear your gym shoes around the house? You might not if you lived in certain countries in Asia! People in these countries believe it's good manners to take off their shoes before they enter a house. Doing this helps keep the house clean. It's also a sign of respect. Showing respect is important no matter where you live.

Be a Super Table Setter!

You have read that it's good manners to help set the table at home. How should you set it? Put out a plate for each person. Then place forks to the left of the plates. Next put knives and spoons to the right of the plates. Just be sure to check with a grown-up before you touch any sharp knives!

Top Five Tips for Good Manners at Home

1. Take turns.
2. Share.
3. Don't speak with your mouth full of food.
4. Offer to help set the table and clear dishes.
5. Don't forget to say "please," "thank you," and "excuse me!"

Glossary

chores—jobs or tasks.

grateful—thankful.

polite—showing good manners by the way you act or speak.

respect—a sign that you care about people or things and want to treat them well.

rude—showing bad manners by the way you act or speak.

situation—the event of a certain moment.

Web Sites

To learn more about manners, visit ABDO Group online at **www.abdopublishing.com**. Web sites about manners are featured on our Book Links page. These links are routinely monitored and updated to provide the most current information available.

Index